FOR _____

FROM _____

DATE _____

*Two are better than one because they have a good reward for their efforts. For if either falls, his companion can lift him up; but pity the one who falls without another to lift him up. Also, if two lie down together, they can keep warm; but how can one person alone keep warm? And if somebody overpowers one person, two can resist him. A cord of three strands is not easily broken.* ~ *Ecclesiastes 4:9–12*

# BIBLE
## PROMISES
### for Couples

Written and compiled by Karen Moore

Copyright © 2014 by B&H Publishing Group

All rights reserved

Printed in China

978-1-4336-8241-4

Published by B&H Publishing Group

Nashville, Tennessee

Dewey Decimal Classification: 242.64

Subject Heading: MARRIED PEOPLE \ DEVOTIONAL
LITERATURE \ CHRISTIAN LIFE

All Scripture quotations are taken from the Holman Christian
Standard Bible®, Copyright © 1999, 2000, 2002, 2003, 2009
by Holman Bible Publishers. Used by permission. Holman
Christian Standard Bible®, Holman CSB®, and HCSB® are
federally registered trademarks of Holman Bible Publishers.

Quotes taken from: *The New Encyclopedia of Christian Quotations*;
published by Baker Books, © 2000 John Hunt Publishing Ltd.
P.O. Box 6287 Grand Rapids, MI 49516-6287 and *The Complete
Guide to Christian Quotations*, © 2011 Barbour Publishing,Inc.,
P.O. Box 719 Uhrichsville, Ohio 44683

1 2 3 4 5 6 7 8 • 18 17 16 15 14

# BIBLE PROMISES

## for Couples

PUBLISHING GROUP
www.BHPublishingGroup.com
NASHVILLE, TENNESSEE

# CONTENTS

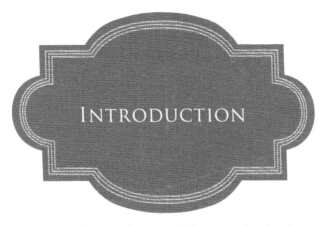

# INTRODUCTION

Two are better than one! By now, you've learned some of the ins and outs of being a couple. Whether you've put years into your relationship, or it's fairly new, you know that being "two" comes with great rewards and a few challenges as well.

God brought you together for a reason. He will invest in your relationship right along with you. He knows that it will take the work of all three of you to make being a couple the gift of love that He intends.

Within these pages, you'll find His promises to be there with you wherever you are. You'll find Scriptures to inspire you as you pray together, quotes from great thinkers to ponder as you discuss life's challenges, and thoughts of love to share with one another. As you open your heart to each other, and open your minds and spirits to God's leading, may you discover even more of the great blessings God had in mind when He chose the two of you to become one. God bless you and keep you forever.

In His Love,
Karen Moore

Always count your blessings, not your troubles.
Always say "I love you," "I'm sorry," and "Thank you."
Always seek the good in each other and in all things.
Practice happiness, laughter, and joy!

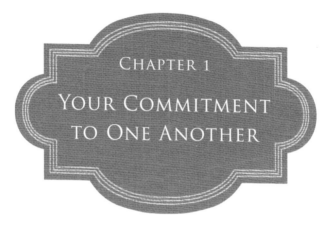

# CHAPTER 1

# YOUR COMMITMENT TO ONE ANOTHER

*Love will teach us all things: but we must learn how to win love; it is gotten with difficulty: it is a possession dearly bought with much labor and over a long time; for one must love not sometimes only, for a passing moment, but always. There is no man who does not sometimes love: even the wicked do that.*
*~ Fyodor Dostoevsky*

The simple truth about love is that it isn't a "once and for all," or even a "one size fits all" kind of thing. Definitions of love are as unique as the two of you are as a couple. That uniqueness offers options that can be played out in a variety of beautiful ways. As Dostoevsky points out here, the kind of commitment to love that couples make is not a sometimes thing. It's an always thing!

If you're going to love your partner "always," you have to fall in love with them over and over again. You have to grow with them and embrace change and respect the little things that make you different from one another. Love is a dynamic and growing experience and as part of a couple, you have every opportunity to give it beauty and balance and depth. Your commitment to love makes all the difference.

## Made for Each Other

> Then the LORD God said, "It is not good for the man to be alone. I will make a helper as his complement." ~ Genesis 2:18

## Your Relationship Is Part of God's Plan

> For we are God's coworkers. You are God's field, God's building. ~ 1 Corinthians 3:9

## Remember the Golden Rule

> Just as you want others to do for you, do the same for them. ~ Luke 6:31

## Monogamy—Cling to Each Other

> I am my love's and my love is mine; he feeds among the lilies. ~ Song of Songs 6:3

## Do Not Be at Odds with Each Other

> Do not take revenge or bear a grudge against members of your community, but love your neighbor as yourself; I am Yahweh. ~ Leviticus 19:18

## Bring Joy to Each Other

> "When a man takes a bride, he must not go out with the army or be liable for any duty. He is free to stay at home for one year, so that he can bring joy to the wife he has married." ~ Deuteronomy 24:5

## Anticipate Each Other with Joy!

Listen! My love is approaching. Look! Here he comes, leaping over the mountains, bounding over the hills. My love is like a gazelle or a young stag. Look, he is standing behind our wall, gazing through the windows, peering through the lattice. My love calls to me. ~ Song of Songs 2:8–10

## Finding a Wife Is a Good Thing!

A man who finds a wife finds a good thing and obtains favor from the Lord. ~ Proverbs 18:22

## What God Has Joined Together

"Haven't you read," He replied, "that He who created them in the beginning made them male and female," and He also said:

"For this reason a man will leave his father and mother and be joined to his wife, and the two will become one flesh?

So they are no longer two, but one flesh. Therefore, what God has joined together, man must not separate." ~ Matthew 19:4–6

## Give Love to Each Other

A husband should fulfill his marital responsibility to his wife, and likewise a wife to her husband. A wife does not have the right over her own body, but her husband does. In the same way, a husband does not have the right over his own body, but his wife does. Do not deprive one another sexually— except when you agree for a time, to devote yourselves to prayer. Then come together again. ~ 1 Corinthians 7:3–5

## Your Commitment to Love

Now as the church submits to Christ, so wives are to submit to their husbands in everything. Husbands, love your wives, just as Christ loved the church and gave Himself for her to make her holy, cleansing her with the washing of water by the word. ~ Ephesians 5:24–26

*God's promises are like stars; the darker the night, the brighter they shine. ~ David Nicholas*

*Constant kindness can accomplish much. As the sun makes ice melt, kindness causes misunderstanding, mistrust and hostility to evaporate. ~ Albert Schweitzer*

*In real love you want the other person's good. In romantic love you want the other person. ~ Margaret Anderson*

*Love is the fulfillment of all our works. There is the goal; that is why we run: we run toward it, and once we reach it, in it we shall find rest. ~ Augustine of Hippo*

*Love does not die easily. It is a living thing. It thrives in the face of all life's hazards, save one—neglect. ~ James D. Bryden*

*The way to love anything is to realize*
*that it might be lost. ~ G. K. Chesterton*

*The most precious possession that ever comes to a person*
*in this world, is the realization that you have won*
*someone's heart. ~ Adapted from Josiah G. Holland*

## God's Love

*Lord, bless the commitment we made to each other*
*as a couple. Help us to honor and love one another in*
*every possible way and to find new reasons to fall in*
*love every day. Strengthen our bonds in our relation-*
*ship and to You, in Jesus' name. Amen.*

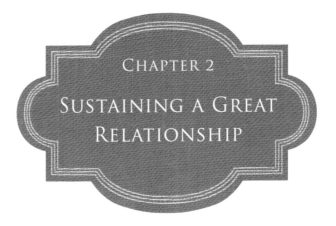

## CHAPTER 2

## SUSTAINING A GREAT RELATIONSHIP

*You'll discover that real love is millions of miles past
falling in love with anyone or anything.*
*~ Sara Paddison*

A current buzz word to discuss a healthy environ-
ment or a flourishing business is to look at whether the
enterprise is "sustainable." If you step back from your
relationship and look at it as a separate entity from the
two of you, almost like a business, what kinds of things
would you assume would be necessary to make your
relationship sustainable? How can you take the stake
you put in the ground when you made a commitment to

each other to make it last, or turn it from good to great, or from ordinary to extraordinary?

Often, people who have been couples for a while realize that they love their partner much more over time than they did when they first started out. They loved those days when they had stars in their eyes and nothing in their heads, but there's something that's much more comfortable and real about all they have shared over time. They've begun to understand what it is about each of them that causes them to fall in love again and again and want to protect their relationship. They've learned how to make their relationship sustainable.

Consider where your focus as a couple is right now. Is the course you're on, one that will ensure a long and happy future? How can God help?

## God Is My Strength

> Yahweh my Lord is my strength; He makes my feet like those of a deer and enables me to walk on mountain heights!
> ~ Habakkuk 3:19

## Honor Your Partner

> "You have heard that it was said, Do not commit adultery. But I tell you, everyone who looks at a woman to lust for her has

already committed adultery with her in
his heart." ~ Matthew 5:27–28

## Husbands and Wives

Husbands, in the same way, live with
your wives with understanding of their
weaker nature yet showing them honor
as coheirs of the grace of life, so that
your prayers will not be hindered.
~ 1 Peter 3:7

## Respect and Love Each Other

Each one of you is to love his wife as
himself, and the wife is to respect her
husband. ~ Ephesians 5:33

## Bear Each Other's Burdens

Carry one another's burdens; in this way
you will fulfill the law of Christ. For if
anyone considers himself to be something when he is nothing, he deceives
himself. ~ Galatians 6:2–3

## Have a Unity of Spirit

Walk worthy of the calling you have received, with all humility and gentleness, with patience, accepting one another in love, diligently keeping the unity of the Spirit with the peace that binds us. ~ Ephesians 4:1–3

## Watch What You Say to Each Other

"I tell you that on the day of judgment people will have to account for every careless word they speak. For by your words you will be acquitted, and by your words you will be condemned." ~ Matthew 12:36–37

## Be Joined to the Lord

They will ask about Zion, turning their faces to this road. They will come and join themselves to the Lord in an everlasting covenant that will never be forgotten. ~ Jeremiah 50:5

## Wherever You Go

Do not persuade me to leave you or go
back and not follow you. For wherever
you go, I will go, and wherever you live,
I will live; your people will be my people,
and your God will be my God. Where
you die, I will die, and there I will be
buried. May Yahweh punish me, and do
so severely, if anything but death sepa-
rates you and me. ~ Ruth 1:16–17

## Commit to The Golden Rule

Therefore, whatever you want others to do for you, do also the same for
them—this is the Law and the Prophets.
~ Matthew 7:12

*To keep your marriage brimming*
*With love in the loving cup,*
*If ever you're wrong, admit it,*
*If ever you're right . . . shut up! ~ Ogden Nash*

*Lord, when we are wrong, make us willing to change.*
*And when we are right, make us easy to live with.*
*~ Peter Marshall*

*A state of mind that sees God in everything*
*is evidence of growth in grace and a thankful heart.*
*~ Charles Finney*

*Love at first is not feeling. Love first can be expressed*
*as giving. That is at the core of love. If one gives, the*
*feeling of love will follow. ~ Jay Adams*

*Gratitude preserves old friendship, and procures new.*
*~ Thomas Fuller*

*Mere change is not growth. Growth is the synthesis of*
*change and continuity, and where there is no continuity*
*there is no growth. ~ C. S. Lewis*

*You can never establish a personal relationship without opening up your own heart. ~ Paul Tournier*

*For anything worth having one must pay the price; and the price is always work, patience, love, self-sacrifice. ~ John Burroughs*

## God's Love

*Lord, help us to desire the kind of relationship that weathers any storm and is sustained through the winds of change that life brings. Help us to grow together and to always seek to make each other a priority. Let us remember our commitment to each other with great joy, looking for fresh ways to make it even stronger with each passing day. Amen.*

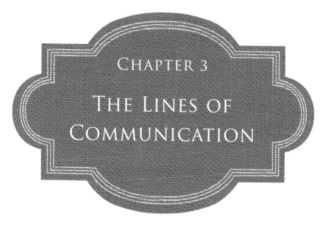

## CHAPTER 3

# THE LINES OF COMMUNICATION

*All married couples should learn the art of battle as they should learn the art of making love. Good battle is objective and honest—never vicious or cruel. Good battle is healthy and constructive, and brings to a marriage the principle of equal partnership.*
*~ Ann Landers*

Some days, it feels like you and your partner can talk about anything. You feel strong and connected. You feel like best friends and the world is open to all kinds of possibilities as you consider the future of your relationship.

Other days, not so much! Other days, you wonder how you got on the same bus, and how you could ever have thought you were going to be able to work together on the trials of life. After all, one of you is creative and one of you is technical. One of you is an optimist and the other one is a realist. You're not the same.

Actually, not being the same is the good news. It's in your differences that you find the best opportunities to create new synergies. It's in the moments of separation that you find a greater desire to come back together. Sometimes you won't agree. Sometimes you'll have to agree to just let a topic go unanswered or unresolved for a while. The key is that you are always willing to walk back through the door, always open to another chance to keep things right between you.

It's been said that couples should not have secrets from each other. Perhaps, but the fact is that the more you know about each other and the more you're willing to talk everything out, the more you will have to build a future and a hope in each other. Communication on every level is one of the ingredients of love. Keep talking!

## Listen

> The mind of the discerning acquires knowledge, and the ear of the wise seeks it. ~ Proverbs 18:15

## A Fitting Word

A man takes joy in giving an answer; and
a timely word—how good that is!
~ Proverbs 15:23

## Reason Together

"Come, let us discuss this," says the
Lord. ~ Isaiah 1:18

## Be Compassionate

The Lord of Hosts says this: "Make fair
decisions. Show faithful love and compassion to one another." ~ Zechariah 7:9

## Rejoice with Each Other

Rejoice with those who rejoice; weep
with those who weep. Be in agreement
with one another. ~ Romans 12:15–16

## God Is With You

I will be with you when you pass through
the waters, and when you pass through
the rivers, they will not overwhelm you.

You will not be scorched when you walk through the fire, and the flame will not burn you. ~ Isaiah 43:2

## Do Good Things

When it is in your power, don't withhold good from the one it belongs to. Don't say to your neighbor, "Go away! Come back later, I'll give it tomorrow"—when it is there with you. ~ Proverbs 3:27–28

## Take Care in What You Say

When there are many words, sin is unavoidable, but the one who controls his lips is wise. The tongue of the righteous is pure silver. ~ Proverbs 10:19–20

## Love Endures

It bears all things, believes all things, hopes all things, endures all things. ~ 1 Corinthians 13:7

## When the Heart Speaks

For the mouth speaks from the overflow
of the heart. A good man produces good
things from his storeroom of good, and
an evil man produces evil things from his
storeroom of evil. ~ Matthew 12:34–35

*The genius of communication is the ability
to be both totally honest and totally kind at the
same time. ~ John Powell*

*Somewhere we know that without silence, words lose
their meaning; that without listening, speaking no
longer heals; that without distance, closeness cannot
cure. ~ Henri Nouwen*

*Let go of your attachment to being right, and suddenly
your mind is more open. You're able to benefit from the
unique viewpoints of others, without being crippled by
your own judgment. ~ Ralph Marston*

*Discussion is an exchange of intelligence; argument is an exchange of ignorance. ~ Unknown Author*

*Eve was not taken from the feet of Adam to be his slave, nor from his head to be his lord, but from his side to be his partner. ~ Peter Lombard*

*He that complies against his will,
Is of his own opinion still. ~ Samuel Butler*

*The deepest principle in human nature
is the craving to be appreciated and the desire
to be important. ~ Dale Carnegie*

*Faith goes up the stairs that love has made and looks out the window that hope has opened. ~ C. H. Spurgeon*

*All who strive for reconciliation seek to listen rather than to convince, to understand rather than to impose themselves. ~ Brother Roger*

*I am certain of nothing but the holiness of the heart's affections, and the truth of imagination. ~ John Keats*

## God's Love

*Father as we work to communicate in better ways with each other, be with us. Help us to speak from the heart and to listen with love. Help us to desire the highest good for each other in all things. Grant that our hopes come to fruition in You and in the mutual efforts we make. Bless our lives together. Amen.*

CHAPTER 4

# YOURS, MINE, AND OURS!

*The mind of Christ is to be learned in the family. Strength of character may be acquired at work, but beauty of character is learned at home. There the affections are trained. ~ Henry Drummond*

When you started your relationship, you had to learn how you wanted to interact as a couple, and how to create time for each of you as individuals. It's important to remember that you also have a responsibility for the outside world and you are a part of God's greater design. You are to care about your neighbors and to volunteer within your community. You have a "family" outside of yourselves and that family also influences the things that happen in your life.

Consider what it means to each of you to step away from your "coupleness" and become a part of the lives of those around you. How does that affect your relationship? How does your involvement in the lives of others shape the way you see your potential and your hopes and dreams?

God brought you together for the sake of each other, but also because He knew that together, you could accomplish things in the world that neither of you could accomplish as well if you were all alone.

See how some of these Scriptures help you understand the bigger picture for your relationship.

## God Provides a Family

> God in His holy dwelling is a father of
> the fatherless and a champion of widows.
> God provides homes for those who are
> deserted. ~ Psalm 68:5–6

## Provide for Each Other

> But if anyone does not provide for his
> own, that is his own household, he has
> denied the faith and is worse than an
> unbeliever. ~ 1 Timothy 5:8

## Heritage of Faith

I thank God, whom I serve with a clear
conscience as my ancestors did, when I
constantly remember you in my prayers
night and day. Remembering your tears, I
long to see you so that I may be filled with
joy, clearly recalling your sincere faith that
first lived in your grandmother Lois, then
in your mother Eunice, and that I am con-
vinced is in you also. ~ 2 Timothy 1:3–5

## Do Good and Share

Don't neglect to do what is good and to
share, for God is pleased with such sacri-
fices. ~ Hebrews 13:16

## Share and Be Friendly

Share with the saints in their needs; pursue hospitality. ~ Romans 12:13

## The Spiritual Mind

The spiritual person, however, can evalu-
ate everything, yet he himself cannot be
evaluated by anyone. For who has known

the Lord's mind, that he may instruct Him? But we have the mind of Christ.
~ 1 Corinthians 2:15–16

## Hand of Fellowship

Since the One at work in Peter for the apostleship to the circumcised was also at work with me for the Gentiles. When James, Cephas, and John, recognized as pillars, acknowledged the grace that had been given to me, they gave the right hand of fellowship to me and Barnabas, agreeing that we should go to the Gentiles and they to the circumcised.
~ Galatians 2:8–9

## Do For Others

Give to everyone who asks from you, and from one who takes away your things, don't ask for them back. Just as you want others to do for you, do the same for them. If you love those who love you, what credit is that to you? ~ Luke 6:30–32

## Love Your Neighbor

Do not take revenge or bear a grudge
against members of your community,
but love your neighbor as yourself; I am
Yahweh. ~ Leviticus 19:18

## Train Up a Child

Teach a youth about the way he should
go; even when he is old he will not
depart from it. ~ Proverbs 22:6

## Don't Be Conformed to this World

Do not be conformed to this age, but
be transformed by the renewing of your
mind, so that you may discern what is the
good, pleasing, and perfect will of God.
~ Romans 12:2

## Bless the Children

Some people were bringing little children to Him so He might touch them,
but His disciples rebuked them. When
Jesus saw it, He was indignant and said

to them, "Let the little children come to Me. Don't stop them, for the kingdom of God belongs to such as these. I assure you: Whoever does not welcome the kingdom of God like a little child will never enter it." After taking them in His arms, He laid His hands on them and blessed them. ~ Mark 10:13–16

*To handle yourself, use your head. To handle others, use your heart. ~ Unknown Author*

*A kind heart is a fountain of gladness making everything in its vicinity freshen into smiles. ~ Washington Irving*

*Inspire little children with your love and laughter and they will awaken the child that still lives within you. ~ K. Moore*

*The best compliment you give a child or a friend*
*is to set them free to make their own choices,*
*to come to right conclusions for themselves,*
*whether or not they coincide with your own.*
*~ Adapted from Alistair Cooke*

*The pain associated with emotional trials*
*and worries can almost always be lessened by a little*
*love. ~ Chris Edmunds*

*There is no exercise better for the heart*
*than reaching down and lifting someone else up.*
*~ Author Unknown*

*Even if it's a little thing, do something for*
*those who have need of help, something*
*for which you get no pay but the privilege of*
*doing it. ~ Albert Schweitzer*

*Hence we must support one another, console one another, mutually help, counsel, and advise. ~ Thomas à Kempis*

*Shared joy is double joy and shared sorrow is half sorrow. ~ Swedish Proverb*

*Patience with others is love,*
*Patience with self is hope,*
*Patience with God is faith. ~ Adel Bestavros*

*Write injuries in dust, benefits in marble.*
*~ Benjamin Franklin*

## God's Love

*Father in Heaven, we thank You for bringing us together. We praise You for helping us to learn more about each other, to strengthen the bonds between us, and the gifts our relationship brings. Help us always to be gracious and kind to each other about the things that affect us individually and as a family. Amen.*

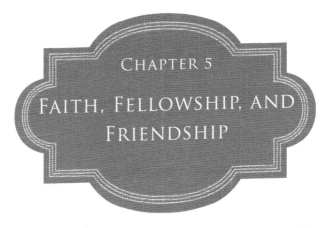

## CHAPTER 5

# FAITH, FELLOWSHIP, AND FRIENDSHIP

*Friendship between the friends of Jesus of Nazareth is
unlike any other friendship. ~ Stephen Neill*

One of the most delightful and enduring aspects
of your life as a couple is the life of faith you share as
well. The fellowship of those in your Bible study or
your church group strengthens and renews your spirit
and helps make your relationship even more sustainable.
There's some truth to the adage that "couples who pray
together, stay together."

When you made a commitment to your relationship, you probably took a leap of faith. You believed in

each other and entrusted your lives to one another's care. That act alone is a remarkable choice to make.

Those who believe that they have been brought together for a purpose, for something outside of their personal relationship, add a dimension to life that is unparalleled. They literally see themselves as a match made in heaven.

How do you now see your mutual faith as an asset to your relationship? How has it helped to sustain you through life's roller coaster events, the ups and downs that all human beings face? As you learn to foster the best in each other and as you come into fellowship at church and in other places with those in your intimate circle, you give God a chance to show you even more of the love He has for you. This is where He offers you an unbreakable and unshakable three-fold cord.

May friends, family, and faith continue to build the bonds of love you share, helping you grow in mutual respect and joy.

## Get Together and Encourage Each Other

Let us hold on to the confession of our hope without wavering, for He who promised is faithful. And let us be concerned about one another in order to promote love and good works, not staying away from our worship meetings, as some habitually do, but encouraging

each other, and all the more as you
see the day drawing near. ~ Hebrews
10:23–25

## The Vine and the Branches

"I am the vine; you are the branches. The
one who remains in Me and I in him
produces much fruit, because you can
do nothing without Me. If anyone does
not remain in Me, he is thrown aside like
a branch and he withers. They gather
them, throw them into the fire, and they
are burned." ~ John 15:5–6

## A Threefold Cord Is Not Easily Broken

Two are better than one because they
have a good reward for their efforts. For
if either falls, his companion can lift him
up; but pity the one who falls without
another to lift him up. Also, if two lie
down together, they can keep warm; but
how can one person alone keep warm?
And if someone overpowers one person, two can resist him. A cord of three
strands is not easily broken.
~ Ecclesiastes 4:9–12

## Believing and Breaking Bread

And they devoted themselves to the apostles' teaching, to the fellowship, to the breaking of bread, and to the prayers. Then fear came over everyone, and many wonders and signs were being performed through the apostles. Now all the believers were together and held all things in common. They sold their possessions and property and distributed the proceeds to all, as anyone had a need. Every day they devoted themselves to meeting together in the temple complex, and broke bread from house to house. They ate their food with a joyful and humble attitude, praising God and having favor with all the people. And every day the Lord added to them those who were being saved. ~ Acts 2:42–47

## Bear with One Another

Now we who are strong have an obligation to bear the weaknesses of those without strength, and not to please ourselves. Each one of us must please his neighbor for his good, to build him up. For even the Messiah did not please Himself. On the contrary, as it is written, The insults of those who insult You have fallen on Me. For whatever was written in the past was written for our instruction, so that we may have hope through endurance and through the encouragement from the Scriptures. Now may the God who gives endurance and encouragement allow you to live in harmony with one another, according to the command of Christ Jesus, so that you may glorify the God and Father of our Lord Jesus Christ with a united mind and voice. Therefore accept one another, just as the Messiah also accepted you, to the glory of God. ~ Romans 15:1–7

## One in Christ

But since that faith has come, we are no longer under a guardian, for you are all sons of God through faith in Christ Jesus. For you are all sons of God through faith in Christ Jesus. For as many of you as have been baptized into Christ have put on Christ like a garment. There is no Jew or Greek, slave or free, male or female; for

you are all one in Christ Jesus. And if you belong to Christ, then you are Abraham's seed, heirs according to the promise.
~ Galatians 3:25–29

## Building on Genuine Love

For this very reason, make every effort to supplement your faith with good-ness, goodness with knowledge, knowl-edge with self-control, self-control with endurance, endurance with godliness, godliness with brotherly affection, and brotherly affection with love. For if these qualities are yours and are increasing, they will keep you from being useless or unfruitful in the knowledge of our Lord Jesus Christ. ~ 2 Peter 1:5–8

## Hold Fast to the Good

For this gospel, I was appointed a her-ald, apostle, and teacher, and that is why I suffer these things. But I am not ashamed, because I know the One I have believed in and am persuaded that He is able to guard what has been entrusted to me until that day. Hold on to the pattern

of sound teaching that you have heard
from me, in the faith and love that are in
Christ Jesus. Guard, through the Holy
Spirit who lives in us, that good thing
entrusted to you. ~ 2 Timothy 1:11–14

## Labor for the Lord

Then He said to His disciples, "The
harvest is abundant, but the workers are
few. Therefore, pray to the Lord of the
harvest to send out workers into His
harvest." ~ Matthew 9:37–38

## Pray in the Spirit and Speak Kindly

Devote yourselves to prayer; stay alert in
it with thanksgiving. At the same time,
pray also for us that God may open a
door to us for the message, to speak the
mystery of the Messiah, for which I am
in prison, so that I may reveal it as I am
required to speak. Act wisely toward
outsiders, making the most of the time.
Your speech should always be gracious,
seasoned with salt, so that you may know
how you should answer each person.
~ Colossians 4:2–6

## You Are Each Part of the Body of Christ

For we were all baptized by one Spirit
into one body—whether Jews or Greeks,
whether slaves or free—and we were
all made to drink of one Spirit. So the
body is not one part but many. If the foot
should say, "Because I'm not a hand, I
don't belong to the body," in spite of this
it still belongs to the body. And if the ear
should say, "Because I'm not an eye, I
don't belong to the body," in spite of this
it still belongs to the body.  If the whole
body were an eye, where would the hearing be? If the whole body were an ear,
where would the sense of smell be? But
now God has placed each one of the parts
in one body just as He wanted. And if they
were all the same part, where would the
body be? Now there are many parts, yet
one body. So the eye cannot say to the
hand, "I don't need you!" Or again, the
head can't say to the feet, "I don't need
you!" But even more, those parts of the
body that seem to be weaker are necessary. And those parts of the body that we
think to be less honorable, we clothe these
with greater honor, and our unpresent-
able parts have a better presentation. But

our presentable parts have no need of clothing. Instead, God has put the body together, giving greater honor to the less honorable, so that there would be no division in the body, but that the members would have the same concern for each other. So if one member suffers, all the members suffer with it; if one member is honored, all the members rejoice with it. Now you are the body of Christ, and individual members of it. ~ 1 Corinthians 12:13–27

## The Reason and Call for Ministry

The One who descended is the same as the One who ascended far above all the heavens, that He might fill all things. And He personally gave some to be apostles, some prophets, some evangelists, some pastors and teachers, for the training of the saints in the work of ministry, to build up the body of Christ, until we all reach unity in the faith and in the knowledge of God's Son, growing into a mature man with a stature measured by Christ's fullness. Then we will no longer be little children, tossed by the waves and

blown around by every wind of teaching,
by human cunning with cleverness in the
techniques of deceit. But speaking the
truth in love, let us grow in every way
into Him who is the head—Christ.
~ Ephesians 4:10–15

## Use Your Gifts for Each Other's Good

Be hospitable to one another without
complaining. Based on the gift each one
has received, use it to serve others, as
good managers of the varied grace of
God. If anyone speaks, it should be as
one who speaks God's words; if anyone
serves, it should be from the strength
God provides, so that God may be glori-
fied through Jesus Christ in everything.
To Him belong the glory and the power
forever and ever. Amen. ~ 1 Peter 4:9–11

*Of all the things which wisdom provides to make us entirely happy, much the greatest is the possession of friendship. ~ Epicurus*

*Is any pleasure on earth as great as a circle of Christian friends by a fire? ~ C. S. Lewis*

*A faithful friend is an image of God. ~ French Proverb*

*The more we love, the better we are, and the greater our friendships are, the dearer we are to God. ~ Jeremy Taylor*

*The glory of friendship is not the outstretched hand, nor the kindly smile, nor the joy of companionship; it is the spiritual inspiration that comes to one when he discovers that someone else believes in him and is willing to trust him with his friendship. ~ Ralph Waldo Emerson*

*There is no wilderness like a life without friends;
friendship multiplies blessings and minimizes
misfortunes; it is a unique remedy against adversity,
and it soothes the soul. ~ Baltasar Gracian*

*Faith is God's work in us that changes us and gives
new birth from God. It kills the Old Adam and makes
us completely different people. It changes our hearts,
our spirits, our thoughts and all our powers. It brings
the Holy Spirit with it. Yes, it is a living, creative,
active and powerful thing this faith. Faith cannot help
doing good works constantly. It doesn't stop to ask if
good works ought to be done, but before anyone asks,
it already has done them and continues to do them
without ceasing. ~ Martin Luther*

## God's Love

*Father, You have designed us for fellowship and
community. We are not meant to live alone and dis-
connected from those around us. We are not meant
to be reclusive even as couples. Help us to be strong
in our friendship with those in our church and our
neighborhood. Help us to always seek to be in continual communion with You and with each other. Amen.*

## CHAPTER 6

## CONFLICT, CHANGE, AND CONTENTMENT

*Hang this question in your houses—"What would Jesus do?" and then think of another—"How would Jesus do it?" For what Jesus would do, and how he would do it, may always stand as the best guide to us.*
~ *C. H. Spurgeon*

Many couples face continual change as the relationship grows, as variables and outside influences find their way to your doorstep. Whether the changes result in conflict or contentment is a matter of discovery and a willingness to come to mutual understanding.

Though the question that Spurgeon poses of "What would Jesus do?" has become almost cliché in recent years, it still holds a remarkable truth. It is a grounded question and takes us outside of personal opinion. It's the one that helps to create opportunity for agreement when you discover you may stand on opposite sides of the fence on a particular issue.

Conflict is a good thing when you know how to use it to your advantage. You can learn from it and grow through it. You can embrace it because it's a great teacher. It can also cause you to feel distant and alienated from each other temporarily as you strive to get back to peace and harmony.

Know that God is with you even in conflict. He is present in your discussions and even your arguments. He knows you seek resolution. He is the author of peace and love and so in all things, offers His help as you seek Him.

Guidance can come through counselors and pastors, friends, and prayer and in love and forgiveness. As you seek to resolve issues as a couple, always stop to consider what Jesus would do and how He might guide you.

## Pearls of Wisdom

> "The kingdom of heaven is like treasure,
> buried in a field, that a man found and
> reburied. Then in his joy he goes and

sells everything he has and buys that
field."

"Again, the kingdom of heaven is
like a merchant in search of fine pearls.
When he found one priceless pearl, he
went and sold everything he had, and
bought it." ~ Matthew 13:44–46

## Give Yourself to the Lord

Deal with Your servant based on Your
faithful love; teach me Your statutes. I am
Your servant; give me understanding so
that I may know Your decrees.
~ Psalm 119:124–125

## Beginning of God's Wisdom

The fear of the LORD is the beginning of
wisdom; all who follow His instructions
have good insight. His praise endures
forever. ~ Psalm 111:10

## Seeking the Lord in Decisions

Now if any of you lacks wisdom, he
should ask God, who gives to all gener-
ously and without criticizing, and it will

be given to him. But let him ask in faith
without doubting. For the doubter is
like the surging sea, driven and tossed by
the wind. That person should not expect
to receive anything from the Lord. An
indecisive man is unstable in all his ways.
~ James 1:5–8

## Knowing God, the True One

And we know that the Son of God has
come and has given us understanding so
that we may know the true One. We are
in the true One—that is, in His Son Jesus
Christ. He is the true God and eternal
life. ~ 1 John 5:20

## The Best Flashlight

Your word is a lamp for my feet and a
light on my path. ~ Psalm 119:105

## Getting a New Heart

I will also sprinkle clean water on you,
and you will be clean. I will cleanse you
from all your impurities and all your
idols. I will give you a new heart and put

a new spirit within you; I will remove
your heart of stone and give you a heart
of flesh. I will place My Spirit within you
and cause you to follow My statutes and
carefully observe My ordinances.
~ Ezekiel 36:25–27

## God Is With You in Your Daily Circumstances

Then the Lord said to Paul in a night
vision, "Don't be afraid, but keep on
speaking and don't be silent. For I am
with you, and no one will lay a hand on
you to hurt you, because I have many
people in this city." ~ Acts 18:9–10

## Building a Beautiful Home

A house is built by wisdom, and it is estab-
lished by understanding; by knowledge
the rooms are filled with every precious
and beautiful treasure. ~ Proverbs 24:3–4

## Building Your House on the Rock

"Therefore, everyone who hears these
words of Mine and acts on them will be

like a sensible man who built his house
on the rock. The rain fell, the rivers rose,
and the winds blew and pounded that
house. Yet it didn't collapse, because its
foundation was on the rock. But everyone who hears these words of Mine and
doesn't act on them will be like a foolish
man who built his house on the sand.
The rain fell, the rivers rose, the winds
blew and pounded that house, and it
collapsed. And its collapse was great!"
When Jesus had finished this sermon, the
crowds were astonished at His teaching.
~ Matthew 7:24–28

## Building Your Relationship on Christ's Foundation

According to God's grace that was given
to me, I have laid a foundation as a
skilled master builder, and another builds
on it. But each one must be careful how
he builds on it. For no one can lay any
other foundation than what has been laid
down. That foundation is Jesus Christ.
~ 1 Corinthians 3:10–11

## Be Content with What You Have

Marriage must be respected by all, and
the marriage bed kept undefiled, because
God will judge immoral people and
adulterers. Your life should be free from
the love of money. Be satisfied with what
you have, for He Himself has said, I will
never leave you or forsake you.
~ Hebrews 13:5–7

## Be Perfectly Joined Together

Now I urge you, brothers, in the name
of our Lord Jesus Christ, that all of you
agree in what you say, that there be no
divisions among you, and that you be
united with the same understanding and
the same conviction. ~ 1 Corinthians
1:10

## Living a Blessed Life

Now finally, all of you should be like-
minded and sympathetic, should love
believers, and be compassionate and
humble, not paying back evil for evil
or insult for insult but, on the contrary,

giving a blessing, since you were called for this, so that you can inherit a blessing.

For the one who wants to love life and to see good days must keep his tongue from evil and his lips from speaking deceit, and he must turn away from evil and do what is good. He must seek peace and pursue it, because the eyes of the Lord are on the righteous and His ears are open to their request. But the face of the Lord is against those who do evil. And who will harm you if you are deeply committed to what is good? But even if you should suffer for righteousness, you are blessed. ~ 1 Peter 3:8–14

## God's Help and Protection

I lift my eyes toward the mountains. Where will my help come from? My help comes from the Lord, the Maker of heaven and earth.

He will not allow your foot to slip; your Protector will not slumber. Indeed, the Protector of Israel does not slumber or sleep.

The LORD protects you; the LORD is a shelter right by your side. The sun will not strike you by day or the moon by night.

The LORD will protect you from all harm; He will protect your life. The LORD will protect your coming and going both now and forever. ~ Psalm 121:1–8

## Don't Let the Sun Go Down on Anger

Since you put away lying, Speak the truth, each one to his neighbor, because we are members of one another. Be angry and do not sin. Don't let the sun go down on your anger, and don't give the Devil an opportunity. ~ Ephesians 4:25–27

## Humble Yourselves Before God

Humble yourselves, therefore, under the mighty hand of God, so that He may exalt you at the proper time, casting all your care on Him, because He cares about you. ~ 1 Peter 5:6–7

## Godliness with Contentment

> But godliness with contentment is a
> great gain. For we brought nothing into
> the world, and we can take nothing out.
> But if we have food and clothing, we will
> be content with these. ~ 1 Timothy 6:6–8

## Remember These Things for the Good of Your Home

> The Lord is near. Don't worry about
> anything, but in everything through
> prayer and petition with thanksgiving, let
> your requests be made known to God.
> And the peace of God, which surpasses
> every thought, will guard your hearts and
> minds in Christ Jesus. Finally brothers,
> whatever is true, whatever is honor-
> able, whatever is just, whatever is pure,
> whatever is lovely, whatever is commend-
> able—if there is any moral excellence
> and if there is any praise—dwell on these
> things. ~ Philippians 4:5–8

*People avoid change until the pain of remaining the same
is greater than the pain of changing. ~ Author Unknown*

*Change is inevitable. Change for the better
is a full-time job. ~ Adlai Stevenson*

*People are always blaming their circumstances
for what they are. The people who get on in this
world are they who get up and look for the
circumstances they want, and, if they can't find
them, make them. ~ George Bernard Shaw*

*Silence is the unbearable repartee. ~ Charles Dickens*

*Contentment is a pearl of great price, and whoever
procures it at the expense of ten thousand desires makes
a wise and happy choice. ~ John Balguy*

*The union of the family lies in love;
and love is the only reconciliation of authority and
liberty. ~ Robert Hugh Benson*

*The most important thing a father can do for his
children is to love their mother. ~ Theodore Hesburgh*

*All the wealth in the world cannot be compared
to the happiness of living together happily united.
~ Margaret of Youville*

## God's Love

*Lord, we thank You for being the same God
yesterday, today, and forever, because we know
that means You are loving us always, that You will
not change. Help us to love each other always even
through change, and even more so, through moments
when we disagree. Bless us so that we are content to
live our best lives together. Amen.*

CHAPTER 7

# FINANCIAL FLARES AND FIZZLES!

*There is no gain except by loss; There is no life except by death; There is no vision but by faith.*
*~ Walter Chalmers Smith*

For most of us, one of life's interchangeable parts is the one that deals with money. Some months, we have it. Other months, we're trying to stretch every dime to make things keep moving along. It's some kind of rocky ship, or uphill climb, or whatever other cliché comes to mind, but it's some kind of unknown.

If fortune smiles upon you, it seems that you actually do well with your savings account and your investments.

But then comes the day in your relationship when one of you is down-sized or re-routed into another whole job market and everything feels confusing and "iffy." You might even get on each other's nerves as you try to figure out just how to deal with the situation that has your resources plummeting and your ideals and dreams along with it.

The good news is that even in the financial flares and fizzles, God remains the best safety deposit box in your account. He never forgets what you need. He never loses sight of the fact that you need to be cared for and sustained in viable ways.

As you look at your own financial picture, remember that it is always subject to change. The only real currency in your bank account is faith and it is always safe in God's hands. That means you're safe too as long as you all stick together.

## Ways to Excel in Life

> Now as you excel in everything—faith, speech, knowledge, and in all diligence, and in your love for us—excel also in this grace. I am not saying this as a command. Rather, by means of the diligence of others, I am testing the genuineness of your love. For you know the grace of our Lord Jesus Christ: Though He was rich,

for your sake He became poor, so that by
His poverty you might become rich.
~ 2 Corinthians 8:7–8

## The Real Secret of Contentment

I rejoiced in the Lord greatly that once
again you renewed your care for me. You
were, in fact, concerned about me, but
lacked the opportunity to show it. I don't
say this out of need, for I have learned to
be content in whatever circumstances I
am. I know both how to have a little, and
I know how to have a lot. In any and all
circumstances I have learned the secret
of being content—whether well fed or
hungry, whether in abundance or in
need. I am able to do all things through
Him who strengthens me. Still, you did
well by sharing with me in my hardship.
~ Philippians 4:10–14

## When Times Are Good

Joseph gathered all the excess food in
the land of Egypt during the seven years
and put it in the cities. He put the food
in every city from the fields around it.

So Joseph stored up grain in such abundance—like the sand of the sea—that he stopped measuring it because it was beyond measure. ~ Genesis 41:48–49

## When Times Are Not Good

Then the seven years of abundance in the land of Egypt came to an end, and the seven years of famine began, just as Joseph had said. There was a famine in every country, but throughout the land of Egypt there was food. Extreme hunger came to all the land of Egypt, and the people cried out to Pharaoh for food. Pharaoh told all Egypt, "Go to Joseph and do whatever he tells you." Because the famine had spread across the whole country, Joseph opened up all the storehouses and sold grain to the Egyptians, for the famine was severe in the land of Egypt. Every nation came to Joseph in Egypt to buy grain, for the famine was severe in every land.
~ Genesis 41:53–57

## Pleasures and Treasures

The one who loves pleasure will become a poor man; whoever loves wine and oil will not get rich. Precious treasure and oil are in the dwelling of the wise, but a foolish man consumes them. The one who pursues righteousness and faithful love will find life, righteousness, and honor. ~ Proverbs 17:17, 20–21

## Commit Your Work to the Lord

All a man's ways seem right to him, but the LORD evaluates the motives. Commit your activities to the LORD and your plans will be achieved. ~ Proverbs 16:2–3

## The Wisdom of the Ant

Go to the ant, you slacker! Observe its ways and become wise. Without leader, administrator, or ruler, it prepares its provisions in summer; it gathers its food during harvest. ~ Proverbs 6:6–8

## Be Prepared and Be Diligent

Know well the condition of your flock, and pay attention to your herds, for wealth is not forever; not even a crown lasts for all time. When hay is removed and new growth appears and the grain from the hills is gathered in, lambs will provide your clothing, and goats, the price of a field; there will be enough goat's milk for your food—food for your household and nourishment for your female servants. ~ Proverbs 27:23–27

## Run for the Prize

Don't you know that the runners in a stadium all race, but only one receives the prize? Run in such a way to win the prize. Now everyone who competes exercises self-control in everything. However, they do it to receive a crown that will fade away. Therefore I do not run like one who runs aimlessly or box like one beating the air. Instead, I discipline my body and bring it under strict control, so that after preaching to others, I myself will not be disqualified. ~ 1 Corinthians 9:24–27

## Working for the Lord

> Whatever you do, do it enthusiastically,
> as something done for the Lord and not
> for men, knowing that you will receive
> the reward of an inheritance from the
> Lord—you serve the Lord Christ.
> ~ Colossians 3:23–24

## Life and Work

> Enjoy life with the wife you love all the
> days of your fleeting life, which has been
> given to you under the sun, all your
> fleeting days. For that is your portion in
> life and in your struggle under the sun.
> Whatever your hands find to do, do with
> all your strength, because there is no work,
> planning, knowledge, or wisdom in Sheol
> where you are going. ~ Ecclesiastes 9:9–10

## Peace to This House

> Whatever house you enter, first say,
> "Peace to this household." If a son of
> peace is there, your peace will rest on
> him; but if not, it will return to you.
> Remain in the same house, eating and

drinking what they offer, for the worker
is worthy of his wages. ~ Luke 10:5–7

## The Rich Man and the Camel

Then Jesus said to His disciples, "I assure
you: It will be hard for a rich person to
enter the kingdom of heaven! Again I tell
you, it is easier for a camel to go through
the eye of a needle than for a rich person
to enter the kingdom of God."
~ Matthew 19:23–24

## Faith and Work

What good is it, my brothers, if someone
says he has faith but does not have works?
Can his faith save him? If a brother or sister
is without clothes and lacks daily food and
one of you says to them, "Go in peace, keep
warm, and eat well," but you don't give
them what the body needs, what good is
it? In the same way faith, if it doesn't have
works, is dead by itself. ~ James 2:14–17

*We live in a world of people struggling to be,
or at least to appear strong, in order not to be weak;
and we follow a gospel which says that when I am weak,
then I am strong. And this gospel is the only thing
that brings healing.* ~ N. T. Wright

*There is nothing wrong with people possessing riches. The
wrong comes when riches possess people.* ~ Billy Graham

*I have made many millions, but they have brought me
no happiness. I would barter them all of the days I sat
on an office stoop in Cleveland and counted myself rich
on three dollars a week.* ~ John D. Rockefeller

*For anything worth having one must pay the price;
and the price is always work, patience, love,
self-sacrifice.* ~ John Burroughs

*I long to accomplish great and noble tasks;*
*but it is my chief duty to accomplish small tasks as if*
*they were great and noble. ~ Helen Keller*

*Far and away the best prize that life offers*
*is the chance to work hard at work worth doing.*
*~ Theodore Roosevelt*

*If you don't excel with talent, triumph with effort.*
*~ Dave Weinbaum*

*I'm very grateful that I was too poor to get to art school*
*until I was 24. . . . I was old enough when I got there to*
*know how to get something out of it. ~ Henry Moore*

*Take courage, and turn your troubles, which are without*
*remedy, into material for spiritual progress. Often turn to*
*our Lord, who is watching you, poor frail little being that you*
*are, amid your labors and distractions. ~ Francis de Sales*

*What then are we to do about problems?*
*We must learn to live with them until such time*
*as God delivers us from them. We must pray for*
*grace to endure them without murmuring. Problems*
*patiently endured will work for our spiritual perfecting.*
*They harm us only when we resist them or endure them*
*unwillingly. ~ A. W. Tozer*

## God's Love

*Father in heaven, You know our needs. You know all the things that we need to navigate life on this planet. You know what we need financially, physically, and spiritually. Help us to look to You and to trust in You in every situation. Help us know that You are with us always. We thank You for Your Divine Providence and Your mercy and love. Amen.*

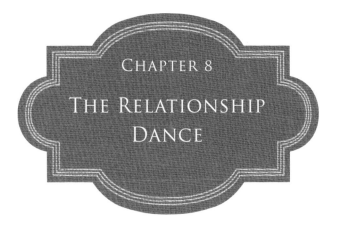

# CHAPTER 8

# THE RELATIONSHIP DANCE

*Two pure souls fused into one by an impassioned love—*
*friends, counselors—a mutual support and inspiration*
*to each other amid life's struggles, must know the*
*highest human happiness; this is marriage;*
*and this is the only cornerstone of an enduring home.*
*~ Elizabeth Cady Stanton*

The beautiful thing about your relationship as a couple is that you get to design it. With God's help, you get to create the roles you will play and how you'll play them within your relationship. You may not always be able to control the circumstances, but you can control your attitude and your response to those circumstances.

The great part of being a couple is that you have a best friend always near you to talk things over and get new perspective. You have someone who is in your corner and who will go to bat for you at a moment's notice. You have a prayer partner and a cornerstone, someone committed to whatever it takes to cause your relationship to blossom and grow. If you don't find these things in each other, what can you do to change the dynamic of your communication?

As you grow together in harmony, honor each other's differences and create the music of your life. May God bless you beyond measure.

## Show Compassion to Each Other

> "The Lord of Hosts says this: Make fair decisions. Show faithful love and compassion to one another." ~ Zechariah 7:9

## Becoming One

> The man gave names to all the livestock, to the birds of the sky, and to every wild animal; but for the man no helper was found who was like him. So the Lord God caused a deep sleep to come over

the man, and he slept. God took one of his ribs and closed the flesh as that place. Then the LORD God made the rib He had taken from the man into a woman and brought her to the man. And the man said: "This one, as last, is bone of my bone, and flesh of my flesh; this one will be called 'woman,' for she was taken from man."

That is why a man leaves his father and mother and bonds with his wife, and they become one flesh. ~ Genesis 2:20–24

## Love Your Wife

Let your fountain be blessed, and take pleasure in the wife of your youth. A loving doe, a graceful fawn—let her breasts always satisfy you; be lost in her love forever. ~ Proverbs 5:18–19

## God's Favor

A man who finds a wife finds a good thing and obtains favor from the LORD. ~ Proverbs 18:22

## A Precious Woman, a Capable Wife

> Who can find a capable wife? She is far more precious than jewels. The heart of her husband trusts in her, and he will not lack for anything good. She rewards him with good, not evil, all the days of her life. ~ Proverbs 31:10–12

## What God Joined Together

> So they are no longer two, but one flesh. Therefore, what God has joined together, man must not separate. ~ Matthew 19:6

## Your Body Is God's Sanctuary

> Don't you know that your body is a sanctuary of the Holy Spirit who is in you, whom you have from God? You are not your own, for you were bought at a price. Therefore glorify God in your body. ~ 1 Corinthians 6:19–20

## Supporting Your Spouse through Faith

> For the unbelieving husband is set apart for God by the wife, and the unbelieving

wife is set apart for God by the husband. Otherwise your children would be corrupt, but now they are set apart for God.
~ 1 Corinthians 7:14

## The Armor of God to Protect You Both

Finally, be strengthened by the Lord and by His vast strength. Put on the full armor of God so that you can stand against the tactics of the Devil. For our battle is not against flesh and blood, but against the rulers, against the authorities, against the world powers of this darkness, against the spiritual forces of evil in the heavens. This is why you must take up the full armor of God, so that you may be able to resist in the evil day, and having prepared everything, to take your stand. Stand, therefore, with truth like a belt around your waist, righteousness like armor on your chest, and your feet sandaled with readiness for the gospel of peace. In every situation take the shield of faith, and with it you will be able to extinguish the flaming arrows of the evil one. Take the helmet of salvation, and

the sword of the Spirit, which is God's
word. ~ Ephesians 6:10–17

## A Note to Husbands and Wives

Wives, be submissive to your husbands,
as is fitting in the Lord. Husbands, love
your wives and don't be bitter toward
them. ~ Colossians 3:18–19

## Full-strength Love

Above all, maintain an intense love for
each other, since love covers a multitude
of sins. Be hospitable to one another
without complaining. ~ 1 Peter 4:8–9

## A Certain Love Story

Boaz took Ruth and she became his wife.
When he was intimate with her, the
Lord enabled her to conceive, and she
gave birth to a son. Then the woman said
to Naomi, "Praise the Lord, who has not
left you without a family redeemer today.
May his name be famous in Israel. He
will renew your life and sustain you in
your old age." ~ Ruth 4:13–15

## The Commandment to Love

This is My command: Love one another as I have loved you. No one has greater love than this, that someone would lay down his life for his friends. You are My friends if you do what I command you.
~ John 15:12–14

*Better communication means an improved relationship.*
*~ Gary Smalley*

*My advice to you is to get married: if you find a good wife you'll be happy; if not, you'll become a philosopher.*
*~ Socrates*

*The marital love is a thing pure as light, sacred as a temple, lasting as the world.*
*~ Jeremy Taylor*

Marriage advice:

- Choose a good spouse.
- Don't marry until you can love entirely.
- Women need affection.
- Take notice of the good things you share.
- Don't magnify imperfections.
- Look for the best in each other.
- Love causes love as fire kindles fire.
- A good husband is the best means to a good and loving wife.
- Be a godly example to each other.

~ Adapted from Richard Baxter


*Life is 10 percent what happens to you, and 90 percent how you respond to it. ~ Chuck Swindoll*

*Every happening, great and small, is a parable whereby God speaks to us, and the art of life is to get the message. ~ Malcolm Muggeridge*

Things to remember as a couple:

- Count your blessings.
- Live one day at a time.
- Say, "I love you."
- Be a giver.
- Seek the good in everything.
- Pray every day.
- Do good deeds for each other.
- Put God first.
- Laugh together.
- Cry together.
- Forgive each other.
- Love each other fiercely.
- Protect and nurture each other.

~ Karen Moore

## God's Love

*Lord, we thank You for bringing us together. We embrace our life as a couple and choose to commit to You and to each other in every circumstance. We choose to laugh together and love together for the rest of our lives, grateful for all that we are and all that we are yet to be. Bless us as a couple and help us to stand on Your promises for us in every way. Amen.*

*The value of compassion cannot be over-emphasized.
Anyone can criticize. It takes a true believer to be
compassionate. No greater burden can be borne by an
individual than to know no one cares or understands.
~ Arthur H. Stainback*

When you became a couple, you probably had nothing but visions of good things, all the happy times you'd share, all the love that you'd give each other, never ending, never running out. You may have thought that no matter what happened in life, you'd be together, able to withstand all that life might bring.

The fact is, that no matter what your story has been, no matter whether it's been a blissful day, or you've wondered if you'd make it through to the next day, you've always had something going for you. You've always had the three-fold cord of God's love for you and your love for each other. Whether your relationship has brought "better or bitter" you've been in it together.

That's the commitment of a great relationship. Be compassionate when times are tough and be grateful when they are not. Your strength as a couple depends on it.

## The Question of Prosperity and Adversity

> In the day of prosperity be joyful, but in the day of adversity, consider: God has made the one as well as the other, so that man cannot discover anything that will come after him. ~ Ecclesiastes 7:14

## The Blessings of a Positive Attitude

> "The poor in spirit are blessed, for the kingdom of heaven is theirs.
>
> Those who mourn are blessed, and they will be comforted.
>
> The gentle are blessed, for they will inherit the earth.
>
> Those who hunger and thirst for righteousness are blessed, for they will be filled.

The merciful are blessed, for they
will be shown mercy.

The pure in heart are blessed, for
they will see God.

The peacemakers are blessed, for
they will be called sons of God.

Those who are persecuted for righteousness are blessed, for the kingdom of
heaven is theirs.

You are blessed when they insult
and persecute you and falsely say every
kind of evil against you because of Me.
Be glad and rejoice, because your reward
is great in heaven. For that is how they
persecute the prophets who were before
you." ~ Matthew 5:3–12

## God's Promises Are a BIG Yes!

For every one of God's promises is "Yes"
in Him. Therefore, the "Amen" is also
through Him by us for God's glory.
Now it is God who strengthens us, with
you, in Christ and has anointed us. He
has also sealed us and given us the Spirit
as a down payment in our hearts.
~ 2 Corinthians 1:20–22

## Giving Up Wealth

"If you want to be perfect," Jesus said to him, "go, sell your belongings and give to the poor, and you will have treasure in heaven. Then come, follow Me." When the young man heard that command, he went away grieving, because he had many possessions. ~ Matthew 19:21–22

## God Will Show You the Way

The Lord will give you meager bread and water during oppression, but your Teacher will not hide Himself any longer. Your eyes will see your Teacher, and whenever you turn to the right or to the left, your ears will hear his command behind you: "This is the way. Walk in it." ~ Isaiah 30:20–21

## Ask Again, Seek Some More, Keep Knocking

"Keep asking, and it will be given to you. Keep searching, and you will find. Keep knocking, and the door will be opened to you. For everyone who asks receives,

and the one who searches finds, and to
the one who knocks, the door will be
opened." ~ Matthew 7:7–8

## The Winning Ways of the Spirit

But the fruit of the Spirit is love, joy,
peace, patience, kindness, goodness, faith,
gentleness, self-control. Against such
things there is no law. Now those who
belong to Christ Jesus have crucified the
flesh with its passions and desires. Since
we live by the Spirit, we must also follow
the Spirit. We must not become con-
ceited, provoking one another, envying
one another. ~ Galatians 5:22–26

## Blessed Assurance of a Clean Heart

Let us draw near with a true heart in full
assurance of faith, our hearts sprinkled
clean from an evil conscience and our
bodies washed in pure water. Let us hold
on to the confession of our hope without
wavering, for He who promised is faithful. And let us be concerned about one
another in order to promote love and
good works. ~ Hebrews 10:22–24

## Speak Kindly to Each Other

> A gentle answer turns away anger, but a harsh word stirs up wrath. The tongue of the wise makes knowledge attractive, but the mouth of fools blurts out foolishness.
> ~ Proverbs 15:1–2

## More Brotherly, Sisterly, and All-the-Time Love

> About brotherly love: You don't need me to write you because you yourselves are taught by God to love one another. In fact, you are doing this toward all the brothers in the entire region of Macedonia. But we encourage you, brothers, to do so even more, to seek to lead a quiet life, to mind your own business, and to work with your own hands, as we commanded you, so that you may walk properly in the presence of outsiders and not be dependent on anyone.
> ~ 1 Thessalonians 4:9–12

## Suffering Creates Stronger Character

And not only that, but we also rejoice in our afflictions, because we know that affliction produces endurance, endurance produces proven character, and proven character produces hope. This hope will not disappoint us, because God's love has been poured out in our hearts through the Holy Spirit who was given to us. ~ Romans 5:3–5

## Forgive Each Other Again and Again

Then Peter came to Him and said, "Lord, how many times could my brother sin against me and I forgive him? As many as seven times?"

"I tell you, not as many as seven," Jesus said to him, "but 70 times seven." ~ Matthew 18:21–22

## Always Bear with Each Other

Therefore, God's chosen ones, holy and loved, put on heartfelt compassion, kindness, humility, gentleness, and patience, accepting one another and forgiving one another if anyone has a complaint against another. Just as the Lord has forgiven you, so also you must also forgive. Above all, put on love—the perfect bond of unity. ~ Colossians 3:12–14

## Sharing a Good Meal

Better a meal of vegetables where there is love than a fattened ox with hatred. ~ Proverbs 15:17

*Once a woman has forgiven her man, she must not reheat his sins for breakfast. ~ Marlene Dietrich*

*The moment an individual can accept and forgive himself, even a little, is the moment in which he becomes to some degree lovable. ~ Eugene Kennedy*

*When you forgive, you in no way change the past—but you sure do change the future. ~ Bernard Meltzer*

*Nothing about our faith makes us pain-proof. It does hurt. It does make us cry. And we must dry our eyes and continue our work until our time is finished.*
*~ Jesse Jackson*

*Call nothing your own, but let everything be yours in common. ~ Augustine*

*In all trouble you should seek God. You should not set him over against your troubles, but within them. God can only relieve your troubles if you in your anxiety cling to him. Trouble should not really be thought of as this thing or that in particular, for our whole life on earth involves trouble; and through the troubles of our earthly pilgrimage we find God. ~ Augustine of Hippo*

*Affection is responsible for nine-tenths of whatever solid and durable happiness there is in our lives. ~ C. S. Lewis*

*Any fact facing us is not as important as our attitude toward it, for that determines our success or failure.*
*~ Norman Vincent Peale*

*The most courageous decision you make each day is the decision to be in a good mood. ~ Voltaire*

*Nothing is really ours until we share it. ~ C. S. Lewis*

## God's Love

*Lord, we've been through a lot together. There have been times when we weren't sure if we would make it, but we did. There have been times when we haven't treated each other with enough love, and yet we've found love again. We are grateful to You for the times we've share, both in joy and in sorrow. We know that You have offered us ways to grow as a couple so that we could be stronger as individuals. Thank You for loving us so much. Amen.*

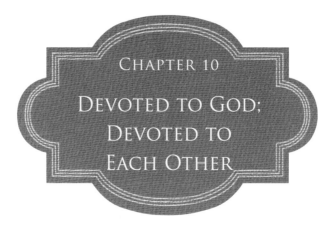

CHAPTER 10

DEVOTED TO GOD;
DEVOTED TO
EACH OTHER

*Every day seek to lose yourself more in Christ, to live
more completely in him, by him, for him, with him.*
*~ C. H. Spurgeon*

No matter how long you've been together, you are
still learning about each other. You learn how to give
more effectively so that your gifts become lasting trea-
sures. You learn your partner's "love language" so you
know better how to please each other.

The same is true of your relationship with God. The more you connect with Him, the more you get to know about Him. You begin to appreciate more fully all that He intends for your life and all that He has for you. You see His hand in all your circumstances and know that you are never alone.

Just as you are devoted to your relationship and to each other, God seeks you to be devoted to Him as well. After all, He devoted His Son to your welfare and to your everlasting good. Offer Him thanks and praise, prayer and communion. Let Him know how excited you are that your life is in His hands. May God bless you and keep you and cause His face to shine upon both of you always. Amen.

## You Are God's Children

> This I proclaim to you. The God who
> made the world and everything in it—
> He is Lord of heaven and earth and
> does not live in shrines made by hands.
> Neither is He served by human hands,
> as though He needed anything, since He
> Himself gives everyone life and breath
> and all things. From one man He has
> made every nationality to live all over
> the whole earth and has determined their
> appointed times and the boundaries of

where they live. He did this so that they might seek God, and perhaps they might reach out and find Him, though He is not far from each one of us. For in Him we live and move and exist, as even some of your own poets have said, "For we are also His offspring." ~ Acts 17:23–28

## Be Still and Know God

"Stop your fighting—and know that I am God, exalted among the nations, exalted on the earth." Yahweh of Hosts is with us; the God of Jacob is our stronghold. ~ Psalm 46:10–11

## Commune with Him

Know that the LORD has set apart the faithful for Himself; the LORD will hear when I call Him. Be angry and do not sin; on your bed, reflect in your heart and be still. ~ Psalm 4:3–4

## Open Your Heart to God

May the words of my mouth and the meditation of my heart be acceptable to

You, Lord, my rock and my Redeemer.
~ Psalm 19:14

## God Is Always Thinking about You

God, how difficult Your thoughts are
for me to comprehend; how vast their
sum is! If I counted them, they would
outnumber the grains of sand; when I
wake up, I am still with You. ~ Psalm
139:17–18

## God's Inspired Word

All Scripture is inspired by God and is
profitable for teaching, for rebuking, for
correcting for training in righteousness,
so that the man of God may be complete,
equipped for every good work.
~ 2 Timothy 3:16–17

## Let Your Light Shine

"You are the light of the world. A city sit-
uated on a hill cannot be hidden. No one
lights a lamp and puts it under a basket,
but rather on a lampstand, and it gives
light for all who are in the house. In the

same way, let your light shine before men, so that they may see your good works and give glory to your Father in heaven." ~ Matthew 5:14–16

## Walking in Love

Therefore I, the prisoner in the Lord, urge you to walk worthy of the calling you have received, with all humility and gentleness, with patience, accepting one another in love, diligently keeping the unity of the Spirit with the peace that binds us. ~ Ephesians 4:1–3

## On Wings of Eagles

He gives strength to the weary and strengthens the powerless. Youths may faint and grow weary, and young men stumble and fall, but those who trust in the Lord will renew their strength; they will soar on wings like eagles; they will run and not grow weary; they will walk and not faint. ~ Isaiah 40:29–31

## Say the Lord's Prayer Often

"Therefore, you should pray like this:
　Our Father in heaven,
　Your name be honored as holy.
　Your kingdom come.
　Your will be done on earth as it is in
　　heaven.
　Give us today our daily bread,
　And forgive us our debts, as we also
　　have forgiven our debtors.
　And do not bring us into temptation,
　　but deliver us from the evil one.
　For Yours is the kingdom and the
　　power and the glory forever.
　Amen." ~ Matthew 6:9–13

## The Throne of Grace

For we do not have a high priest who
is unable to sympathize with our weaknesses, but One who has been tested
in every way as we are, yet without sin.
Therefore let us approach the throne
of grace with boldness, so that we may
receive mercy and find grace to help us
at the proper time. ~ Hebrews 4:15–16

## Draw Near to God with a True Heart

Therefore, brothers, since we have boldness to enter the sanctuary through the blood of Jesus, by a new and living way that He has opened for us through the curtain (that is, His flesh), and since we have a great high priest over the house of God, let us draw near with a true heart in full assurance of faith, our hearts sprinkled clean from an evil conscience and our bodies washed in pure water. Let us hold on to the confession of our hope without wavering, for He who promised is faithful. ~ Hebrews 10:19–23

## Perfect Love Takes Away Our Fear

There is no fear in love; instead, perfect love drives out fear, because fear involves punishment. So the one who fears has not reached perfection in love. We love because He first loved us. ~ 1 John 4:18–19

## Ask for God's Help

Now this is the confidence we have before Him: Whenever we ask anything according to His will, He hears us. And if we know that He hears whatever we ask, we know that we have what we have asked Him for. ~ 1 John 5:14–15

## God Is Your Ever-Present Help

My help comes from the LORD, the Maker of heaven and earth. He will not allow your foot to slip; your Protector will not slumber. ~ Psalm 121:2–3

## A Strong Spirit

For God has not given us a spirit of fearfulness, but one of power, love, and sound judgment. ~ 2 Timothy 1:7

## God's Incredible Love

The one who does not love does not know God, because God is love. God's love was revealed among us in this way: God sent His One and Only Son into the world so that we might live through Him. Love consists in this: not that we loved God, but that He loved us and sent

His Son to be the propitiation for our sins. ~ 1 John 4:8–10

## Things to Remember When You're Distressed

Now we have this treasure in clay jars, so that this extraordinary power may be from God and not from us. We are pressured in every way but not crushed; we are perplexed but not in despair; we are persecuted but not abandoned; we are struck down but not destroyed.
~ 2 Corinthians 4:7–9

## Grace and Peace

Peace to the brothers, and love with faith, from God the Father and the Lord Jesus Christ. Grace be with all who have undying love for our Lord Jesus Christ.
~ Ephesians 6:23–24

Put on the full armor of God so that you can stand against the tactics of the Devil. For our battle is not against flesh and blood, but against the rulers, against the authorities, against the world powers of this darkness, against the spiritual forces of evil in the heavens. This is why you must take up the full armor of God, so that you may be able to resist in the evil day, and having prepared everything, to take your stand. ~ Ephesians 6:11–13

*True and living devotion presupposes the love of God.*
*~ Francis de Sales*

*We should dedicate ourselves to becoming in this life the most perfect worshipers of God we can possibly be, as we hope to be through all eternity. ~ Brother Lawrence*

*God is not moved or impressed with our worship until our hearts are moved and impressed by Him. ~ Kelly Sparks*

*Praising God is one of the highest and purest acts of religion. In prayer we act like men; in praise we act like angels. ~ Thomas Watson*

*Gratitude is born in hearts that take time to count up past mercies. ~ Charles Jefferson*

*God, I give you the praise for days well spent. But I am yet unsatisfied, because I do not enjoy enough of You. I apprehend myself at too great a distance from You. I would have my soul more closely united to You by faith and love. ~ Susanna Wesley*

*The Glory of God, and, as our only means to glorifying Him, the salvation of human souls, is the real business of life. ~ C. S. Lewis*

*For worship is a thirsty land crying out for rain, It is a candle in the act of being kindled, It is a drop in quest of the ocean . . . It is a voice in the night calling for help, It is a soul standing in awe before the mystery of the universe . . . It is time flowing into eternity . . . A man climbing the altar stairs to God. ~ Dwight Bradley*

*The Glory of God, and, as our only means to glorifying Him, the salvation of human souls, is the real business of life. ~ C. S. Lewis*

*Open wide the windows of our spirits and fill us full of light; open wide the door of our hearts, that we may receive and entertain Thee with all our powers of adoration. ~ Christina Rossetti*

*The most fundamental need, duty, honor and happiness of mankind is not petition, nor even contrition, nor again even thanksgiving—these three kinds of prayer which, indeed, must never disappear out of our spiritual lives—but adoration. ~ Von Hugel*

## God's Love

*Lord, we love you! We worship You with all that we are and all that we have. We thank You for bringing us together as a couple. We thank You for guiding and leading and providing for all we need. With humble hearts, we lift up our arms to You in praise and adoration. Amen.*

## CHAPTER 11

## IT TAKES ALL KINDS OF LOVE TO MAKE YOUR WORLD GO ROUND

*I remember the morning that I first asked the meaning of the word "love . . ." Miss Sullivan put her arm gently round me and spelled into my hand, "I love Helen." "What is love?" I asked . . . "Love is something like the clouds that were in the sky before the sun came out," she replied. "You cannot touch the clouds, you know; but you feel the rain and know how glad the flowers and the thirsty earth are to have it after a hot day. You cannot touch love either; but you feel the sweetness that it pours into everything. Without love you would not be happy or want to play."*
*~ Helen Keller*

As a couple, you continue to define *love* for yourselves. You notice it shaping itself around experiences that draw you closer together, or around moments that find you drawing the same heartfelt conclusions. You realize that the people around you may not share love in the same ways that you do, because you have created something unique and special for yourselves.

Love is at once something you can hold and something that holds you. It keeps you centered and grounded and offers you the freedom to go and become what you're meant to be. No doubt, love has definitions you haven't even discovered yet, but if you're open to it and willing to give it an opportunity, you'll see it unfold in new ways all the time. Love is what makes your relationship new with each sunrise because "you feel the sweetness it pours into everything" the longer you're together.

## Put On Love

> Therefore, God's chosen ones, holy and loved, put on heartfelt compassion, kindness, humility, gentleness, and patience, accepting one another and forgiving one another if anyone has a complaint against another. Just as the Lord has forgiven you, so also you must forgive. Above all, put on love—the perfect bond of unity.
> ~ Colossians 3:12–14

## Accept One Another

> Therefore I, the prisoner in the Lord, urge you to walk worthy of the calling you have received, with all humility and gentleness, with patience, accepting one another in love, diligently keeping the unity of the Spirit with the peace that binds us. ~ Ephesians 4:1–3

## Growing Older Together

> Older men are to be level headed, worthy of respect, sensible, and sound in faith, love, and endurance. In the same way, older women are to be reverent in behavior, not slanderers, not addicted to much wine. They are to teach what is good, so that they may encourage the young women to love their husbands and children, to be self-controlled, pure, homemakers, kind, and submissive to their husbands, so that God's message will not be slandered. ~ Titus 2:2–5

## Love and Your Inheritance

For God is not unjust; He will not forget your work and the love you showed for His name when you served the saints—and you continue to serve them. Now we want each of you to demonstrate the same diligence for the final realization of your hope, so that you won't become lazy but will be imitators of those who inherit the promises through faith and perseverance. ~ Hebrews 6:10–12

## Love and Trials

A man who endures trials is blessed, because when he passes the test he will receive the crown of life that God has promised to those who love Him. No one undergoing a trial should say, "I am being tempted by God." For God is not tempted by evil, and He Himself doesn't tempt anyone. But each person is tempted when he is drawn away and enticed by his own evil desires. ~ James 1:12–14

## Gaining Wisdom

But the wisdom from above is first pure, then peace-loving, gentle, compliant, full of mercy and good fruits, without favoritism and hypocrisy. And the fruit of righteousness is sown in peace by those who cultivate peace. ~ James 3:17–18

## Love Covers Many Sins

Above all, maintain an intense love for each other, since love covers a multitude of sins. Be hospitable to one another without complaining. Based on the gift each one has received, use it to serve others, as good managers of the varied grace of God. ~ 1 Peter 4:8–10

## Be Aware of a Love for the World

Do not love the world or the things that belong to the world. If anyone loves the world, love for the Father is not in him. For everything that belongs to the world—the lust of the flesh, the lust of the eyes, and the pride in one's lifestyle—is not from the Father, but is from the world. And the world with its lust is passing away, but the one who does God's will remains forever. ~ 1 John 2:15–17

## Another Definition of Love

Dear friends, if our conscience doesn't condemn us, we have confidence before God and can receive whatever we ask from Him because we keep His commands and do what is pleasing in His sight. Now this is His command: that we believe in the name of His Son Jesus Christ, and love one another as He commanded us. The one who keeps His commands remains in Him, and He in him. And the way we know that He remains in us is from the Spirit He has given us. ~ 1 John 3:21–24

## Remain In His Love

God is love, and the one who remains in love remains in God, and God remains in him. ~ 1 John 4:16

## Perfect Love

In this, love is perfected with us so that we may have confidence in the day of judgment, for we are as He is in this world. There is no fear in love; instead, perfect love drives out fear, because fear involves punishment. So the one who fears has not reached perfection in love. We love because He first loved us.
~ 1 John 4:17–19

*To my God a heart of flame;*
*To my fellow man a heart of love;*
*To myself a heart of steel.*
*~ Augustine of Hippo*

*We are able to love others only when we love ourselves.*
*~ Brent A. Barlow*

*He alone loves the Creator perfectly who manifests pure love for his neighbor. ~ Venerable Bede*

*Know this: though love is weak and hate is strong, yet hate is short, and love is very long.* ~ Kenneth Boulding

*It is astonishing how little one feels poverty when one loves.* ~ John Bulwer

*Sometimes it's a form of love just to talk to somebody that you have nothing in common with and still be fascinated by their presence.* ~ David Byrne

*Anything will give up its secrets if you love it enough. Not only have I found that when I talk to the little flower or to the little peanut they will give up their secrets, but I have found that when I silently commune with people they give up their secrets also—if you love them enough.* ~ George Washington Carver

*Love is not a thing of enthusiastic emotion. It is a rich, strong, vigorous expression of the whole round Christian character—the Christ-like nature in its fullest development. And the constituents of this great character are only to be built up by ceaseless practice.*
*~ Henry Drummond*

*Ecstasy cannot last, but it can carve a channel for something lasting. ~ E. M. Forster*

*Nature teaches us to love our friends, but religion our enemies.~ Thomas Fuller*

*Love never claims, it ever gives; love never suffers, never resents, never revenges itself. Where there is love there is life; hatred leads to destruction.*
*~ Mahatma Gandhi*

*We look forward to the time when the power
to love will replace the love of power.
Then will our world know the blessings of peace.*
*~ William Gladstone*

*Love has the power to give in a moment, what toil can
scarcely reach in an age. ~ Goethe*

*Whoever loves, allows themselves willingly to be
corrected, without seeking excuses, in order to be freer
in love. ~ Hadewijch of Brabant*

*The soul that walks in love neither tires others nor
grows tired. ~ John of the Cross*

*Love does not make the world go round.
Love is what makes the ride worthwhile.
~ Franklin P. Jones*

*Love gives itself; it is not bought.*
*~ Henry Wadsworth Longfellow*

*What power can poverty have over a home where loving*
*hearts are beating with a consciousness of untold riches of*
*the head and the heart? ~ Orison Swett Marden*

*Love me when I least deserve it, because that's when I*
*really need it. ~ Swedish proverb*

*She sat and wept, and with her untressed hair*
*She wiped the feet she was blest to touch;*
*And He wiped off the soiling despair*
*From her sweet soul—because she loved so much.*
*~ Dante Gabriel Rossetti*

*Love is . . .*
*Swift,*
*Sincere,*
*Pious,*
*Joyful,*
*Generous,*
*Strong,*
*Patient,*
*Faithful,*
*Prudent,*
*Long-suffering,*
*Courageous,*
*And never seeking its own;*
*For wherever a person seeks his own,*
*There he falls from love.*
*~ Thomas à Kempis*

## God's Love

Lord, we recognize that You have created us to love, and not simply to love ourselves, but to love You and to love others with full hearts. We ask that You would widen our understanding of all that it means to truly love each other. Help us to desire more of the kind of love You would have us know. We ask this in the name of Jesus. Amen.

## CHAPTER 12

## IT'S ALL IN THE HEART OF FORGIVENESS

*In a dream, Martin Luther once had he saw a book where his sins were written. In the dream, the devil spoke to Luther, "Martin, here is one of your sins, here is another," pointing to the writing in the book. Then Luther said to the devil, "Take a pen and write, "The blood of Jesus Christ, God's Son, cleanses us from all sin." ~ Martin Luther*

Whether we wrestle with the need to be forgiven by someone else, or the need to forgive someone ourselves, the fact remains that we only can recognize true forgiveness through our relationship with Jesus Christ. It is and will always be a matter of the heart. As a couple, you surely realize those moments when lack of forgiveness is the elephant in the room. It is the one thing that may be difficult, but must be addressed.

When you start with the understanding that God forgives you as you forgive each other, it helps to bring the healing and the opportunity you may need to genuinely and lovingly forgive each other. When you lay your sins at the foot of the cross, you'll find the strength to seek the forgiveness you need. Help each other to forgive, to love, and to grow beyond those things that may temporarily separate your hearts from one another.

## Pardon Our Wrongdoing

> "So now, may My Lord's power be magnified just as You have spoken: The Lord is slow to anger and rich in faithful love, forgiving wrongdoing and rebellion. But He will not leave the guilty unpunished, bringing the consequences of the father's wrongdoing on the children to the third and fourth generation. Please pardon the wrongdoing of this people, in keeping with the greatness of Your faithful love, just as You have forgiven them from Egypt until now." ~ Numbers 14:17–19

## The Happiness of Knowing You're Forgiven

How joyful is the one whose transgression is forgiven, whose sin is covered! How joyful is the man the LORD does not charge with sin and in whose spirit is no deceit!

When I kept silent, my bones became brittle from my groaning all day long. For day and night Your hand was heavy on me; my strength was drained as in the summer's heat. Then I acknowledged my sin to You and did not conceal my iniquity. I said, "I will confess my transgressions to the LORD," and You took away the guilt of my sin. ~ Psalm 32:1–5

## God Is Ready to Forgive You

For You, Lord, are kind and ready to forgive, rich in faithful love to all who call on You. LORD, hear my prayer; listen to my plea for mercy. I call on You in the day of my distress, for You will answer me. ~ Psalm 86:5–7

## Forgiveness Up to High Heaven

> For as high as the heavens are above the earth, so great is His faithful love toward those who fear Him. As far as the east is from the west, so far has He removed our transgressions from us. As a father has compassion on his children, so the LORD has compassion on those who fear Him. For He knows what we are made of, remembering that we are dust.
> ~ Psalm 103:11–14

## Those Big Sins Are Forgiven Too

> "Come, let us discuss this," says the LORD. "Though your sins are like scarlet, they will be as white as snow; though they are as red as crimson, they will be like wool." ~ Isaiah 1:18

## God Forgives All Your Mistakes

> "It is I who sweep away your transgressions for My own sake and remember your sins no more." ~ Isaiah 43:25

## What Happens When You Forgive Each Other

> "For if you forgive people their wrong-doing, your heavenly Father will forgive you as well. But if you don't forgive people, your Father will not forgive your wrongdoing." ~ Matthew 6:14–15

## Jesus Forgives and Heals

> Just then some men brought to Him a paralytic lying on a mat. Seeing their faith, Jesus told the paralytic, "Have courage, son, your sins are forgiven."
>
> As this, some of the scribes said among themselves, "He's blaspheming!"
>
> But perceiving their thoughts, Jesus said, "Why are you thinking evil things in your hearts? For which is easier: to say, 'Your sins are forgiven,' or to say, 'Get up and walk'? Bot so you may know that the Son of Man has authority on earth to forgive sins"—then He told the paralytic, "Get up, pick up your mat, and go home." And he got up and went home. ~ Matthew 9:2–7

## The Unforgivable Sin

"I assure you: People will be forgiven for all sins and whatever blasphemies they may blaspheme. But whoever blasphemes against the Holy Spirit never has forgiveness, but is guilty of an eternal sin"—because they were saying, "He has an unclean spirit." ~ Mark 3:28–29

## The Prayer that Brings Forgiveness

"Therefore, I tell you, all the things you pray and ask for—believe that you have received them, and you will have them. And whenever you stand praying, if you have anything against anyone, forgive him, so that your Father in heaven will also forgive you your wrongdoing. But if you don't forgive, neither will your Father in heaven forgive your wrongdoing." ~ Mark 11:24–26

## The Measure of Forgiveness

"Do not judge, and you will not be judged. Do not condemn, and you will not be condemned. Forgive, and you will be forgiven. Give, and it will be given to you; a good measure—pressed down, shaken together, and running over—will be poured into your lap. For with the measure you use, it will be measured back to you." ~ Luke 6:37–38

## Hold On to This Message

Let the message about the Messiah dwell richly among you, teaching and admonishing one another in all wisdom, and singing psalms, hymns, and spiritual songs, with gratitude in your hearts to God. And whatever you do, in word or in deed, do everything in the name of the Lord Jesus, giving thanks to God the Father through Him. ~ Colossians 3:16–17

## God Strengthens Your Heart

My flesh and my heart may fail, but God is the strength of my heart, my portion forever. ~ Psalm 73:26

## Request for Forgiveness

> May You hear in heaven, Your dwelling
> place, and may You forgive and repay the
> man according to all his ways since You
> know his heart, for You alone know the
> human heart, so that they may fear You
> and walk in Your ways all the days they
> live on the land You gave our ancestors.
> ~ 2 Chronicles 6:30–31

*The most tremendous judgment of God in this world is
the hardening of the hearts of people. ~ John Owen*

*Neither prayer, nor praise, nor the hearing of the word
will be profitable to those who have left their hearts
behind them. ~ C. H. Spurgeon*

*The only place trespassers are truly forgiven is in
church. ~ K. Moore*

*Two works of mercy set a person free: forgive and you will be forgiven, and give and you will receive.*
*~ Augustine of Hippo*

*Forgiveness is the answer to the child's dream of a miracle by which what is broken is made whole again, what is soiled is again made clean.*
*~ Dag Hammarskjold*

*God has cast our confessed sins into the depths of the sea, and He's even put a "No Fishing" sign over the spot.*
*~ D. L. Moody*

*The moment an individual can accept and forgive himself, even a little, is the moment in which he becomes to some degree lovable. ~ Eugene Kennedy*

*When you forgive, you do not change the past, but you certainly change the future. ~ Bernard Meltzer*

*A humble heart is a forgiving heart. ~ K. Moore*

*Forgiveness Breaks Down the Walls of Bitterness
Bitterness imprisons life, love releases it.
Bitterness paralyzes life; love empowers it.
~ Harry Emerson Fosdick*

*Bitterness sickens life; love heals it.
Bitterness blinds life; love anoints its eyes.
~ Harry Emerson Fosdick*

*It is very difficult and expensive to undo after you are married, the things your parents did to you while you were putting your first six birthdays behind you.
~ Bureau of Social Hygiene study 1928*

## God's Love

*Lord, thank You for showing us the healing power of forgiveness. Help us to be willing to listen carefully to each other and to lovingly forgive each other. Help us to not only forgive those things that have caused us pain, but to release them to You so that we may remember them no more. Remind us how often we require forgiveness ourselves either from You or from others we love. Help us to hold fast to the things that are good for us, letting go of those things that no longer serve us well. We ask for your continual forgiveness in our lives both as individuals and as a couple. Amen.*